RUDOLF STEINER called his spiritual philosophy 'anthroposophy', meaning 'wisdom of the human being'. As a highly developed seer, he based his work on direct knowledge and perception of spiritual dimensions. He initiated a modern and universal 'science of spirit', accessible to anyone willing to exercise clear and unprejudiced thinking.

From his spiritual investigations Steiner provided suggestions for the renewal of many activities, including education (both general and special), agriculture, medicine, economics, architecture, science, philosophy, religion and the arts. Today there are thousands of schools, clinics, farms and other organizations involved in practical work based on his principles. His many published works feature his research into the spiritual nature of the human being, the evolution of the world and humanity, and methods of personal development. Steiner wrote some 30 books and delivered over 6000 lectures across Europe. In 1924 he founded the General Anthroposophical Society, which today has branches throughout the world.

Only where sense knowledge ends
stands the doorway opening
the soul to living realities;
the soul creates the key
when it grows strong within itself
through struggle which worldly forces wage
on their own ground with
human powers;
when by its own means soul drives off
the sleep that at the senses' furthest limit
shrouds powers of knowledge in spiritual night.

WHITSUN
AND ASCENSION

Festivals

Also available:

(Festivals)
Christmas
Easter
Michaelmas
St John's

(Practical Applications)
Agriculture
Architecture
Art
Education
Eurythmy
Medicine
Religion
Science
Social and Political Science

(Esoteric)
Alchemy
Atlantis
Christian Rozenkreutz
The Druids
The Goddess
The Holy Grail

RUDOLF STEINER

WHITSUN
AND ASCENSION
An Introductory Reader

Compiled with an introduction,
commentary and notes by
Matthew Barton

Sophia Books

Sophia Books
An imprint of Rudolf Steiner Press
Hillside House, The Square
Forest Row, RH18 5ES

www.rudolfsteinerpress.com

Published by Rudolf Steiner Press 2007

For earlier English publications of individual selections please
see pp. 109–10

The material by Rudolf Steiner was originally published in
German in various volumes of the 'GA' (*Rudolf Steiner
Gesamtausgabe* or Collected Works) by Rudolf Steiner Verlag,
Dornach. This authorized volume is published by permission of
the Rudolf Steiner Nachlassverwaltung, Dornach (for further
information see pp. 113–14)

All translations revised by Matthew Barton

*Matthew Barton would like to thank Margaret Jonas, librarian at Rudolf
Steiner House, for her invaluable help in locating volumes used in
compiling this book.*

This selection and translation © Rudolf Steiner Press 2007

A catalogue record for this book is available from the British
Library

ISBN 978 185584 169 7

Cover by Andrew Morgan
Typeset by DP Photosetting, Neath, West Glamorgan
Printed by Cromwell Press Ltd., Trowbridge, Wiltshire

Contents

Introduction

The age-old differences of view between Jewish and Christian tradition often conceal deep parallels, sympathies and similarities. In Jewish tradition, the festival of Shavu'ot falls very close to the Christian Pentecost. One of its many dimensions, besides celebrating the giving of the Torah, or body of sacred teachings, to the Jews, is a celebration of the 'first fruits' of harvest. In many places in this volume Rudolf Steiner speaks of flowers and fruit, and in particular of Whitsun as the 'fruit' of Easter: of a culminating point when a gift given universally to all humanity can ripen into the seed of individual insight in each separate one of us. This culmination reminds me of the 'dew point' when dew condenses out of the atmosphere; and in fact it used to be a Pentecost tradition to walk barefoot through dew-covered meadows before Whit Sunday mass, and to feed one's animals bread soaked in this dew.

In this volume Steiner has much to say about the seed power in imaginative pictures. I want to explore these images of dew and fruit a little further, for they seem to me to illuminate Whitsun and Ascension.

A drop of dew reflects the cosmos in its globed shape and in the way it gathers light and shines, almost as though it were a small sun itself. In his poem entitled 'On a Drop of Dew', Andrew Marvell writes how the dewdrop

Does, in its pure and circling thoughts, express
The greater heaven in an heaven less.

Marvell compares the dewdrop to the human soul, that is 'divided from the sphere' it originally came from. 'Trembling, lest it grow impure', the dewdrop must wait

Till the warm sun pity its pain,
And to the skies exhale it back again.

While Marvell's dewdrop is one that shuns the darker reaches of the material world and, unlike most human souls in our day and age, is eager to 'dissolve' and 'run / Into the glories of the almighty sun', the image nevertheless conjures a sense of the soul's potential kinship with elevated spiritual and cosmic realities. None of us can claim the pure transparency and urge for transcendence of Marvell's dewdrop. Most probably we would not want to, since we intuitively feel a need to engage fully with the physical world. Nevertheless, we can probably recognize the yearning for a purer state, an ascent to unearthly existence. The evaporating dewdrop clearly relates to Ascension, to sublimation into another condition. This is both a beautiful image of death, but also, if we strive to 'dissolve' too soon, a warning that this might be merely escape, a failure to complete what we came here for. To complement it we need another picture, which Whitsun gives us.

The word *Dichter* in German is translated as 'poet' but literally means someone who 'condenses' what is ineffable and inarticulate into speech. T. S. Eliot spoke of poetry as a 'raid on the inarticulate'[1] and Robert Frost wrote: 'A poem begins as a lump in the throat, a homesickness, a lovesickness. It finds the thought and the thought finds the words.'[2] So here we can sense a condensation or dewpoint where words descend upon us. But descending is not enough. A poet must at the same time work his way towards the 'Muse', must labour to make himself sensitive and permeable enough to clothe the impalpable Word in words, render himself a vessel to bear the spirit that wants to speak through him. Steiner refers to this reversal of direction many times: the moment of culmination when what has been prepared in us through our own efforts sends a spark of current, of connection, allowing the immaterial realm to infuse and manifest in us. This is also why Whitsun can be felt as a 'fruit' or harvest of the spiritual gifts whose real significance comes from their internalization in us. A fruit of course is itself a wonderful image of this 'enclosure' and maturation of gifts, and of their life-bearing potency.

Think of a sunflower, a member of the large *Compositae* family. Each flowerhead is a single whole yet simultaneously a community of many small, individual florets. Like all flowers, of course, it first opens utterly to the sun. It drinks in solar forces, and even turns during the day to follow the sun's course through the heavens. Its countenance, the flower disc, faithfully reflects the sun's image. The gesture, though, is not simply one of receiving but of reaching upwards as far as possible, of active transmutation into substance of what is received, of bringing down and condensing subtle, ethereal realities into fruit and seed. Someone once demonstrated to me something that, conceptually, I initially refused to believe: that light is actually invisible and only manifests where it meets earthly resistance.[3] The community of sunflower florets transforms invisible light into matter, with the power to germinate life. In the same way the circle of disciples at Whitsun—as an archetypal image of all human fraternity—makes immanent and individual the descending Holy Spirit in separate tongues of a single fire, and then carries these flames of inspiration into the world.

'Speaking in tongues', as Steiner makes clear, is a metaphor for heartfelt words that communicate directly with other human beings, irrespective of race, creed, nationality or any other of the divisions which, like an annoying tinnitus, so easily interfere with our perception and 'reception' of them. Words can be empty husks or they can be tempered into a power that seeds others' hearts. If they do so they can begin to create an expanding, universal humanity in which each single individual is embedded in the whole without losing his distinct and separate qualities.

In a world fraught with increasingly divergent and dogmatic viewpoints, in which (often) all seem to be warring with all, what could be more vital in both senses of the word than a festival that celebrates not conflicting viewpoints but the shared dewpoint where spirit manifests on earth?

The passages and extracts collected here are just that—longer or shorter extracts from the larger context of whole lectures. Steiner developed his lectures into an art form in the best sense, and the reader is referred to the original, complete lectures for the 'total experience' and context from which these passages are drawn.

Matthew Barton

RISING TO THE CLOUDS, TETHERED TO EARTH

1. Blossoming to Bear Fruit

Extract from a lecture given in Dornach on
7 May 1923

*Time lapse photography can reveal the wonderful rhythm
of flowers opening and closing in quick motion, reminiscent of the systole and diastole of the human heart.
Here Steiner directly relates flower and heart, embodied
in the opening expansion of Ascension and Whitsun's
contraction to a 'fruit' in which the human spirit's fire-
tempered seed flickers dynamically.*

When people strive again to fill the course of the
year with spiritual understanding for the festival
seasons, the seasons will be imbued once more with
real cosmic significance. Within earthly existence
human beings will learn to accompany and
experience cosmic existence.

Whitsun is also pre-eminently a festival of
flowers. Whoever has a true feeling for this festival
will go out among the buds and blossoms opening
under the sun's influence, under etheric and astral
influences,[4] and will perceive in the flower-decked

earth the earthly image and reflection of what streams together in the two pictures of Christ's Ascension and the descent of the tongues of fire upon the heads of the disciples. The opening human heart may be symbolized by the flower opening to the sun; and what pours down from the sun, giving the flower the fertilizing power it needs to bear fruit, may be symbolized by the tongues of fire descending upon the heads of the disciples. Anthroposophy[5] can work upon human hearts with the power that streams from an understanding of the festivals, and from true contemplation of each festival season; it can help evoke the mood of soul that truly belongs to these spring days.

2. Release from Bondage: a Festival of Awareness

Extract from a lecture given in Berlin, Whit Monday, 23 May 1904

To continue the picture of flower and fruit, Ascension is seen here as a transfiguration of the body, much as the flower is a culmination and transformation of a plant's green leaves. This utter unfolding is followed, like out-breath by inbreath, by the impetus and capacity for renewed life: in the case of Whitsun in the form of higher, more conscious realization.

Thus the Easter mystery is only revealed in its fullness when taken together with the mystery of Whitsun. We see the human ego,[6] exemplified in its divine representative, divesting itself of the lower ego and dying in order for its physical nature to be completely transfigured and offered up again to the Godhead. Ascension is the pictorial symbol of this. When we have transfigured the physical body and offered it up again to the spirit, we will be ripe to receive the influx of spiritual life, to experience what is called the 'coming of the Holy Spirit', in the words of humanity's greatest, archetypal representative ...

The human spirit should be free and not dull or constrained. That is also Christianity's deepest aim. Health and healing are connected with holiness. A spirit that is holy can heal. Human beings released from bondage to their physiological state are healthy and free ...

Thus Whitsun can be seen as the symbol of the emancipation of the human spirit, as the great symbol of humanity's struggle for freedom, and for consciousness of our freedom.

If the Easter festival is the festival of resurrection in nature, then the Whitsun festival is the symbol of the human spirit becoming conscious, the festival of those who know and understand, and who, thoroughly imbued by this awareness, go in search of freedom ...

We must see clearly what binds us to our physical surroundings but also what connects us with what is invisible within nature. We have to know where we stand. For we human beings are not confined to a dull, dreamy, half-life, but are destined to develop a free, fully conscious unfolding of our whole being.

3. Penetrating the Pictures

Extract from a lecture given in Dornach on
7 May 1923

*Here Steiner appeals to his listeners to conjure vivid
pictures of both Ascension and Whitsun. Such imaginative pictures, unlike fixed concepts, can be endlessly
deepened and enhanced, and have a living quality. A new
aspect of Ascension that Steiner describes here is as a
warning of dissolution – of flower without fruit perhaps –
which Christ's deed counteracted. He also distinguishes
between Easter that represents a physical redemption of all
humanity, and Whitsun as a festival of the individualized
insight needed to carry humanity forwards. Such insight
is the 'spirit seed' that forms in each separate one of us.
Dynamic thinking, as typified by living, imaginative
pictures, is needed to develop our individual capacities of
knowledge, which can reconnect each of us again with all
other human beings, the earth and the cosmos.*

People think that they get to the bottom of a subject
just by grasping a concept. No such view is possible
in the case of a picture or imagination, which works

in a living way, like a living being, like a human being even. Whatever aspects of a living being we come to know, it will keep presenting new aspects to us. We will not be satisfied with supposedly comprehensive definitions but will keep looking for characteristics that enlarge our picture, giving us steadily increasing knowledge.

Today I want to present you with two familiar pictures, and describe certain aspects of them.

The first picture is that of the disciples of Jesus Christ on the day of the Ascension. Gazing upwards they see Christ vanishing into the clouds. The usual interpretation of this scene is that Christ ascended to heaven and so departed from the earth, and that the disciples—and indeed all humanity for whose sake Christ fulfilled the Mystery of Golgotha—were then left to their own resources.

It may occur to you that in a certain respect this belies the reality of the Mystery of Golgotha. We know that through his Deed on Golgotha[7] Christ resolved to unite his own being with the earth—in other words, to remain forever connected with earth evolution from then on. The mighty picture of the Ascension might therefore seem at odds with what esoteric vision of the Mystery of Golgotha reveals about Christ's union with the earth and humanity. Today let us try to draw on the spiritual facts to resolve this apparent contradiction.

The second picture I would like you to imagine is that of the scene ten days after the Ascension, when tongues of fire descend upon the heads of the assembled disciples and they are moved to 'speak with other tongues'. This means, in fact, that the disciples were then able to impart the secrets of the deed on Golgotha to the hearts of all human beings, irrespective of religion and creed.

Keep these two pictures in mind as we try to give some indication of their meaning ...

In his book *The Face of the Earth*, Eduard Suess has stated that the soil beneath our feet today belongs to an earth that is already dying. During the Atlantean epoch[8] the earth was, so to say, in its mid-life period; it teemed with inner life and had no such formations as the rocks and stones of our times, which are gradually eroding. The mineral element was active in the earthly realm in the way in which it is active today in an animal organism, in a state of solution out of which deposits will not form unless the organism is diseased. If the animal organism is healthy it is only the bones that can be said to take their form as deposits. There is still however inner life in the bones — they are not crumbling into dust like our mountains and rocks. This erosion and crumbling is evidence that the earth is already succumbing to a death process ... The human physical body is involved in the earth's process of decline ...

At about the time of the Mystery of Golgotha, the human physical body had reached such a degree of decline that those who were then in incarnation[9] or who would be incarnated in the near future (up to about the fourth century AD) were faced with an earth that was growing dangerously desolate and barren, in which in future they would be unable to descend from the soul-spiritual world to build a physical body from earthly substance. This danger existed, and the inevitable consequence would have been the human being's failure to fulfil his allotted earthly mission. By the time of the Mystery of Golgotha, the combined ahrimanic and luciferic powers[10] had succeeded in bringing humanity close to the point of extinction.

Humanity was rescued from this fate, was healed, by the Mystery of Golgotha. The human physical body itself was imbued again with the necessary forces of life and vitality. Human beings were given the capacity to continue their further evolution on earth, could now descend from soul-spiritual worlds and find it possible to live in physical bodies. Such was the very real effect of the Mystery of Golgotha ...

Turning now to the biblical event, to the picture of the Ascension, we must realize that at that time the disciples had become clairvoyantly able to behold what is, in truth, a deep secret of earthly evolution.

These secrets remain unnoticed by people's everyday consciousness, which is incapable of knowing whether at one point or another in human evolution something of supreme importance is taking place ... The picture of the Ascension actually signifies that at this moment Christ's disciples were able to witness an event of great significance, enacted as it were behind the scenes of evolution.

What they witnessed revealed to them a picture, a prospect of what would have come about for humanity if the Mystery of Golgotha had not taken place. They beheld the vivid spiritual reality of what would then have occurred. They saw that human physical bodies would have deteriorated so radically that humanity's whole future would have been at risk. The consequence of this physical deterioration would have been that the human etheric body[11] would have obeyed the forces of attraction that properly belong to it. The etheric body is continually being drawn sunwards, not earthwards. Our physical body has earthly weight, subject to gravity, but our etheric body has the opposite, what one might call 'levity'. Had the human physical body degenerated, as it inevitably would without the Mystery of Golgotha, human etheric bodies would have followed their untethered attraction towards the sun and have left the physical body, thus bringing to an end humanity's existence on earth.

Until the Mystery of Golgotha, Christ's dwelling place was the sun. As the human etheric body strives towards the sun, therefore, it is striving towards Christ. Now picture to yourselves the Ascension scene: in spiritual vision the disciples see Christ himself rising heavenwards. A vision is conjured before them of how the human being's etheric nature, in its upward striving, unites itself with the power and impulse of Christ. The human etheric body, which was in danger of forsaking the earth and being drawn out towards the sun, like dispersing clouds, is instead held together and contained by Christ through the Mystery of Golgotha. This picture must be rightly understood for it is actually a warning. Christ is akin to those forces in us that naturally strive towards the sun and away from the earth, and will always do so. But Christ remains in union with the earth, thus keeping us securely tethered to it.

In this picture of the Ascension, therefore, the disciples perceived what would have happened if the Mystery of Golgotha had not taken place ... Christ rescued for the earth our sunward-striving etheric body. The fact that Christ grasps and contains what strives sunwards shows that he remains united with humanity on earth. Through the Mystery of Golgotha, Christ enacted a cosmic event within Earth evolution. He descended from heights of spirit, linked himself with humanity in the man Jesus of Nazareth, fulfilled the Mystery of Golgotha and united his evolution with that of the earth. It was a cosmic deed accomplished for all humanity ...

The Christ deed on Golgotha is an objective fact whose cosmic significance does not depend on what we believe about it. An objective fact has independent reality. If an oven is hot, it does not become cold because a number of people believe it to be so. The Mystery of Golgotha rescues humanity from the decline of the physical body, no matter what people believe or do not believe about it ...

It is therefore now possible for human beings to find on earth bodies into which they can and will, for long future ages, be able to incarnate. It is, however, as beings of *spirit and soul* that human beings pass through life in these now rejuvenated human bodies on earth. As beings of spirit and soul they can appear on the earth again and again. And the Christ impulse, which must have significance for the human being's spiritual nature as well as for his physical body, can impress itself upon our waking condition but not enter our sleep life unless we receive this impulse into our soul.

The Mystery of Golgotha therefore produced its effect in the waking life of those who had no knowledge of it, but it fails to affect them in their sleep life. The inevitable result of this will be that while human beings have gained the possibility of incarnating time and again on earth, without *knowledge* of the Mystery of Golgotha the condition of their sleep will become such that the connection of their spirit and soul nature with Christ will eventually fade ... To take effect in our spirit and soul, the Christ impulse must also penetrate the human soul during sleep—something only possible if we consciously acknowledge the significance of the Mystery of Golgotha. The spiritual effect of the Mystery of Golgotha can only proceed from *awareness of its meaning*.

Humanity must therefore come to realize that, on the one hand, Christ holds back the etheric body in its perpetual urge towards the sun, but, on the other, that our spirit and soul nature, the ego and astral body,[12] can receive the Christ impulse only in the period between falling asleep and awaking—something only possible when knowledge of this impulse has been acquired consciously in waking life.

Let us therefore picture the Ascension scene yet again. The disciples have a clairvoyant vision of the sunward-streaming flow of human etheric bodies, but they also perceive how Christ unites himself with this urge, restrains it and tethers it. The mighty scene of the Ascension is that of the rescue of the human being's physical and etheric nature by Christ.

The disciples withdraw in deep contemplation, for in their awakened souls is the knowledge that through the Mystery of Golgotha the physical and etheric nature of mankind as a whole has been preserved. But what happens, they wonder, to the spirit and soul? Where do human beings acquire the power to receive the Christ impulse into their spirit and soul, into their ego and astral body? The answer is found in the Whitsun festival.

Through the Mystery of Golgotha the Christ impulse has taken effect on the earth as a reality which can only be perceived and grasped by spiritual cognition. Materialistic knowledge and science cannot approach it, and so the soul must acquire the power of spiritual cognition, spiritual perception, spiritual feeling, in order to be able to understand how, on Golgotha, the Christ impulse was united with earthly impulses.

Christ Jesus fulfilled the deed of Golgotha for this purpose, in such a way that ten days after the event of Ascension he sent the human being the pos- sibility of also imbuing his inner soul-spiritual nature, his ego and astral body, with the Christ impulse. Permeation of the human spirit and soul with the power to understand the Mystery of Gol- gotha, the sending of the Holy Spirit, is the picture of the Whitsun festival, of Pentecost. Christ fulfilled his deed for all humanity, but to each human individual who understands this deed Christ sent the spirit. He gave the spirit and soul of each individual access to what was accomplished for all mankind. Through the spirit we must learn to experience the Christ mystery inwardly, in spirit and soul.

Thus these two pictures stand side by side in humanity's evolution. The Ascension picture tells us that the deed of Golgotha was fulfilled for the physical body and the etheric body in the universal human sense, while Whitsun tells us that each single human being must make this deed bear fruit in himself by receiving the Holy Spirit. The Christ impulse is thereby individualized in each human being.

And now we can add something else to the picture of the Ascension. Spiritual visions, such as came to the disciples on the day of Ascension, always have a bearing on what we can experience in a particular state of consciousness. After death, as you know, the etheric body leaves the human being. We lay aside the physical body at death, retaining the etheric body for a few days, and then the etheric body dissolves, and actually unites with the sun. In this dissolution after death we unite with solar forces streaming through the realms of space—which also contain the earth. Since the Mystery of Golgotha we can behold both this departing etheric body and the Christ who rescued it for future earthly existence. Since the Mystery of Golgotha there stands before the soul of every human being who passes through death the Ascension picture which the disciples in their particular soul-state were able to behold that day.

But for those who also imbue their being with the Whitsun mystery, who allow the Holy Spirit to draw near, this picture after death becomes the source of the greatest consolation they can possibly experience, for now they behold the Mystery of Golgotha in its full truth and reality. This picture of the Ascension tells them: 'You can confidently entrust all your subsequent incarnations to Earth evolution, for Christ has become the Saviour of this evolution through the Mystery of Golgotha.'

For those whose ego and astral body do not penetrate to the essence of the Mystery of Golgotha, this picture becomes an admonition until they too learn to understand it. After death this picture urges them to acquire for their next earthly life the forces that will enable them to understand and penetrate the Mystery of Golgotha. That this picture of the Ascension should, initially, stand there as a kind of admonition is only natural, for in subsequent earthly lives human beings can then strive to invoke the forces they have been urged to acquire, and thus begin to grasp the significance of the Mystery of Golgotha ...

This should convey to you something of the mood of soul in which a true feeling for the festivals of Ascension and Whitsun can arise. The pictures which such festivals bring before the soul are like living beings: we can never exhaust their reality, can always discover more in them ...

SUFFERING'S OPENING DOOR

4. No Celebration but Truth

Extract from a lecture given in Berlin on 6 June 1916

Here Steiner warns against detaching ourselves from the world's suffering, even in a festival celebration. Festivals, and pre-eminently Whitsun, need to include all humanity rather than shielding us from harsh realities. Whitsun calls on us to connect with the world by developing a new, non-materialistic way of thinking.

Mankind is passing through fateful ordeals and at such times it is not always possible to call upon uplifting, heart-warming feelings. If our feelings are right and true we can never for a single moment forget the suffering of our times, and in a certain sense it is actually selfish to wish to forget it and to give ourselves up to thoughts that warm and uplift the soul ... Our recent studies have shown very clearly that many of the reasons for the sufferings of the present time lie in prevailing attitudes and ways of thought, and that it is vitally urgent to help the human soul develop so that humanity can progress to better times ...

For those who seek the spirit, this Whitsun festival has a meaning and content of special profundity, calling for continual renewal of the spiritual quest.

In our days it is necessary that such festival thoughts should go deeper than at other times. How we emerge from the grievous events of these times will depend very largely on the degree to which people can experience these thoughts. People are already starting to realize that they will have to work their own way out of the present catastrophic conditions we find ourselves in, through inner effort. And those who come to spiritual science should feel, still more intensely, the need to surmount materialism. This victory over materialism will only be possible if we have the will to kindle the world of spirit into living activity within us, to celebrate the Whitsun festival inwardly and with true earnestness.

5. The Struggles of Prometheus

Extract from a lecture given in Berlin on Whit
Monday, 23 May 1904

*In Greek mythology the figure of Prometheus – who stole
fire from the Gods and brought it to humanity, and was
punished for this by Zeus with endless torments – is an
embodiment of the human struggle for freedom from
physical bondage. Before the tongues of spiritual fire can
descend in an inner Whitsun, we have to battle our way
through suffering, loss and loneliness.*

Through the figure of Prometheus Greek mythology has symbolized free humanity struggling
towards culture. He is the representative of suffering mankind, but at the same time the giver of
freedom. The one who sets Prometheus free is
Heracles, of whom it is said that he underwent
initiation in the Eleusinian Mysteries. Whoever
descended to the underworld was an initiate, for
this descent is a technical term, as it were, denoting
initiation. Such journeys to the underworld are
attributed to Heracles, Odysseus and all who are

initiates, who wished to lead the human being of those times to the source of primeval wisdom, to a life of spirit.

[Our modern] materialistic culture shows us how far human beings have become embedded in their purely physical and physiological nature. But it is equally certain that the vulture, the symbol of lust and craving gnawing at our liver, will be thrust aside by those who seek the spirit ...

The human being lives primarily in his lower organism, in his consciousness imbued with desires. It is right that this is so, because it is only this consciousness which can give him an awareness of his true goal — to attain freedom. He should not remain there, however, but must raise his ego to the nature of spirit, bring it to birth so that it becomes a spirit of healing — a Holy Spirit ...

The highest goal of humanity is symbolically expressed in the Whitsun festival: humanity must progress once more from a merely intellectual to an authentic life of spirit. Just as Prometheus was set free from his suffering by Heracles, so will humanity be liberated by the power of the spirit. By descending into matter we have attained conscious self-awareness. By ascending again we will become self-aware spirits ...

6. Gain Only Through Loss: All Knowledge Born from Pain

Extract from a lecture given in Christiania (Oslo) on 17 May 1923

Drawing out yet another thread of the picture, Steiner focuses here on a tension in the period from Ascension to Whitsun. From loss of the faculty of vision, given as a gift, the disciples pass through a dark night of grief and loneliness. It is only because of this that the direction of inspiration and impetus is reversed: from external influx to emanation from within. Their grief tempers the soul and renders it an inward vessel to contain their own inspired activity, kindling a spark of connection to the Holy Spirit from which humanity has been so long sundered.

We must cast our minds back to earlier ages when human consciousness was altogether different from that of today. Three or four thousand years ago human beings were instinctively aware that before coming down into a physical body on earth they had lived in the world of spirit. Every individual in those times knew that within him was a being of soul and spirit sent down into earth existence by divine powers. Human consciousness of death was also different; in those days people could remember their pre-earthly, soul-spiritual existence, and knew that the part of them that had lived before this earthly life would also live on beyond death.

In those days there were schools of learning which were at the same time religious institutions — the mysteries as they are called — where people were instructed in knowledge about life before birth. By means of such teachings they came to realize that before their earthly existence they had lived among stars and beings of spirit, just as on earth they were now living among plants and animals, mountains and rivers ...

The mysteries taught people that before they descend to earth the sublime sun being gives them power enabling them to return to the spiritual world, the world of stars, in the right way after death ... The hymns and devotional exercises directed towards the sun had a particularly strong influence on human feeling and soul life. People felt themselves united with the divine universe when they participated in sun worship ...

It was known to the initiated priests of these mysteries that the sublime sun spirit of whom they spoke to the worshippers was the same being as he who would later be called Christ. But before the Mystery of Golgotha the priests had to say: 'If you wish to know something of the Christ you will seek in vain on earth; you must raise yourselves up to find the secrets of the sun, for only outside and beyond the earth will you fathom the mysteries of Christ.'

It was relatively easy for people at that time to accept such teaching because they had instinctive memory of the realm of Christ from which they had descended to earth. But human nature is involved in a process of evolution and this instinctive recall of pre-earthly, spiritual life was gradually lost. Eight hundred years before the Mystery of Golgotha there were only a very few in whom any instinctive memory of pre-earthly life still survived... It was as if people on earth had been wholly forsaken by the Christ power, were no longer able to kindle to life within them any memory of the spiritual worlds.

Then for the first time what may be called the fear of death overshadowed humanity. When people of former times saw the physical body die they knew that souls belong to the kingdom of Christ and do not die. But now they were greatly troubled about the destiny of the immortal, eternal being within them. It was as though the link between themselves and the Christ had been severed. This was because they were no longer able to look up into worlds of spirit, and in the earthly realm Christ was nowhere to be found.

Then at the time when human beings could no longer find the Christ, on the far side of the sun in the realm of spirit, out of infinite grace and mercy Christ came down to earth so that humanity might find him there. What happened then in the evolution of the universe has no parallel with anything within the range of human knowledge ... Since human beings could no longer reach him, Christ came to them on earth. To do this it was necessary that he should undergo what no divine power had ever previously undergone: birth and death. Christ became the soul of a man, Jesus of Nazareth, and passed through birth and death ...

With the help of anthroposophical[13] knowledge we can carry ourselves back in imagination to the time when Christ Jesus walked in Palestine and lived through his earthly destiny. We can look into the hearts of the disciples and apostles who realized intuitively that the being whose abode was once the sun had descended to earth and dwelt among them... Therefore these disciples said to themselves: 'Out of the eyes of Jesus of Nazareth the light of the sun rays forth to us. Out of the words of Jesus of Nazareth streams the power of the warmth-giving sun. When Jesus of Nazareth moves among us it is as though the sun itself is sending its light and power into the world.'

Those who could understand this said: 'Moving among us in the form of a man is the sun being whom in earlier times people could reach only by directing their gaze upwards from the earth to the world of spirit.' And because the disciples and apostles knew this, their attitude to Christ's death was also true and right; and they could remain disciples of Christ Jesus even after he had passed through death on the earth.

Spiritual science enables us to know that when Christ had departed from the body of Jesus of Nazareth he moved in a spiritual form among his disciples and continued to teach them. A power had been given to the apostles and disciples that enabled them to continue to receive the teaching of Christ when he appeared to them in this spiritual body. However this power left them after a certain time. There came a point in the lives of the disciples when they said to themselves: 'We have seen him but we now see him no longer. He came down from heaven to us on earth. Where has he gone?

The point when the disciples believed they had again lost the presence of Christ is commemorated in the Christian festival of Ascension. This is a remembrance of the disciples' conviction that the sublime sun being who had walked the earth in the man Jesus of Nazareth had vanished from their sight. At this loss the disciples were overwhelmed with a sorrow that cannot be compared with any other sorrow on earth ...

All real knowledge, all knowledge that can truly be called great, is born from pain, from inner travail. When people pursue the path towards knowledge, into the higher worlds, as described in the anthroposophical science of the spirit, the goal can only be reached by passing through pain. Without suffering intensely, and thus freeing one-self from pain's oppression, no one can gain knowledge of the world of spirit.

During the ten days following the Ascension the suffering of Christ's disciples was beyond all tell-ing, because Christ had vanished from their sight. And out of this pain, out of this infinite sorrow, there sprang what we call the mystery of Pentecost, the Whitsun mystery. Having lost the sight of Christ in instinctive, outward clairvoyant vision, the disciples found it again in their inmost being, feelings and inner experience—found it again through sorrow and pain ...

The disciples of Christ turned their thoughts to all that their memory had preserved of the event of Golgotha. And out of this memory, and the suffer-ing it evoked, a vision arose in their souls of what humanity had lost because it no longer possessed the faculty of instinctive clairvoyance. People of old had said: 'Before we were born on earth we dwelt with Christ. From him we have the power which leads to immortality.' And now, ten days after they had lost outer vision of Christ, the disciples said: 'We beheld the Mystery of Golgotha and this gives us the power to feel again the reality of our immortal being.' This is expressed symbolically by the tongues of fire at Pentecost. Thus spiritual science illumines the Pentecost secret: the Mystery of Golgotha has replaced the sun myths of the ancient mysteries ...

If we truly understand Christianity we know that the sun shines upon all mankind. It shines on Thebes, Olympia and Mecca. Physically the sun can be seen in the same way everywhere. So too, the sublime sun being, the Christ, can be worshipped spiritually everywhere. Anthroposophy shows that the being who before the Mystery of Golgotha could be reached only by instinctive, supersensory faculties can since then be reached through a power of knowledge acquired on the earth itself ...

People will again come to understand ... that the being whose dwelling place used to be the sun is now to be found on earth ... and dwells among human beings in the sphere of earth. They will be able to continuously re-experience what the disciples experienced as the Whitsun mystery: Christ has descended to earth, and a power that guarantees our immortality is dawning in our hearts ...

But this means that through the science of the spirit we must again learn to perceive a spiritual reality in everything that is of a material nature: a spiritual reality underlying stones, plants, animals, human beings; a spiritual reality underlying the clouds, the stars, the sun. When we penetrate what is material and find in it the spirit in all its dynamic reality once again, we also open our soul to the voice of Christ—who will speak to us if we are willing to hear him ...

This is what anthroposophy wishes to bring humanity as a perpetual Whitsun mystery. And when, prepared by anthroposophy, people are ready to seek for the spiritual world again, they will find Christ as an ever-present reality in the way that is wholly appropriate to the needs of our age. If, in our times, people do not turn to spiritual knowledge, they will lose Christ. Until now Christianity did not depend upon knowledge. Christ died for all human beings. He did not deny them. But if in our times people reject knowledge of Christ, then they deny him ...

People today need to turn not merely to dead words but to knowledge which actually leads them to the light in which the living Christ dwells: not the historical figure who dwelt on earth centuries ago, but the Christ who lives now and will live through all future times among human beings, because he who was once their God has become their divine brother ...

ALL ONE TO ALONE TO ONE
IN ALL

7. Forming a Conscious Vessel

Extract from a lecture given in Cologne on
7 June 1908

In this lecture Steiner as it were 'ascends' from the vital forces and beings at work in nature through the unified group souls of animals to the separate and potentially isolated human ego. This 'advance', though, is at the same time a descent into matter and loss of connection with the living world of spirit. From this deepest point, reflected in the loss of vision between Ascension and Whitsun, we need to find access to what Steiner calls the 'higher group soul' of the Holy Spirit, which reunites us in enhanced spiritual awareness.

The spiritual evolution of humanity for which we strive must bring us into a living connection with the whole surrounding world. A great deal of what surrounds us, for which our forefathers still felt awe and wonder, now strikes many people as dead and prosaic. There is for example a widespread feeling of alienation towards our seasonal festivals; the urban population in particular has largely lost sight of the significance of Christmas, Easter and Whitsun. People no longer feel connected, as in earlier times, with the mighty content of the festivals, nor do they have much insight into what these reflect of the great realities of the world of spirit. Nowadays people feel cold and prosaic towards Christmas, Easter and, especially, Whitsun. The pouring down of the spirit has become for many a mere abstraction, which will only regain truth and life when people once more develop a truly spiritual knowledge of the whole world.

Much is said nowadays about the forces of nature but very little about the beings behind those forces. Our forefathers spoke of gnomes, undines, sylphs and salamanders, but nowadays people regard this as just old-fashioned superstition. It does not matter much, in itself, what theories people hold, but when their theories blind them to certain realities, when they begin to apply these theories in practical life, this has more serious repercussions.

When people say that their ancestors' beliefs in gnomes, undines, sylphs, salamanders and the like was all nonsense, one feels like replying: 'Well go and ask the bees.' If bees could speak they would tell us that the sylphs are no superstition; bees know what they owe to them. Anyone whose eyes of spirit are open can discover what force draws bees towards flowers. 'Natural instinct' is an empty phrase. Actual beings, which our ancestors called sylphs, are active in bee swarms, and lead the bees to blossom to seek sustenance.

It is especially where the different kingdoms of nature come into contact with each other that various different kinds of elemental beings reveal themselves: within the bowels of the earth, where rock and veins of metal ore meet; at a spring, where moss spreads upon stone, so that plant and mineral kingdoms come into contact; or where plant and animal meet (for example where a bee enters a flower); and also where the human being and the animal encounter one another. But in the latter case such beings do not appear in the mundane encounters of everyday life, for instance when a butcher slaughters an ox or someone eats meat. They appear, rather, when two realms meet in an excess and outpouring of life forces. In particular they arise where someone has the kind of relationship with animals which particularly engages his thoughts and feelings. A shepherd, for example, may have this kind of special connection with his sheep. Such feeling connections were very common in former times, resembling the relationship which an Arab has to his horse, rather than that of a racing-stable owner. When soul forces play over from one realm into another — as they do between a shepherd and his lambs, or when effusions of smell and taste stream from the flowers towards the bees—certain beings find an opportunity to incarnate. The spiritual investigator perceives a small aura around the edge of the blossoms when bees thrust their way into them and suck. The bee in the flower becomes a medium of taste and streams out a kind of flower aura which nourishes the sylphs. In the same way salamanders are nourished by the feelings weaving between shepherd and sheep...

If opportunities are provided to nourish such beings then they appear. When, for example, human beings allow evil thoughts to stream out from themselves, certain elemental beings are drawn into their aura, finding nourishment there...

If we think further about it we must realize that we are wholly surrounded by beings of spirit. Each breath of wind, every breeze is more than mere chemical substance. It is also the revelation of such beings who encircle and permeate us. If we are not, in the future, to suffer a very sad and constricting fate, we must know what lives around us. We cannot progress without such knowledge. We must ask ourselves how these beings arise and where they come from. Such a question will help us begin to understand how certain harmful and evil elements can be transformed and made good through the wise guidance of higher worlds. Think of manure or dung as a metaphor of this. It is excreted as a waste product, yet it can have a beneficial effect if we make good use of it as the basis for new plant growth. Things that have seemingly been left behind by evolving life can be retrieved and transformed by higher powers. This is very much the case with those beings we have been speaking of . . .

Salamanders are beings which need a certain kind of relationship between man and animal. Human beings alone, of all creatures on earth, possess an ego enclosed within themselves; animals on the other hand have a group ego or group soul. This means that all the animals of a particular species share a common ego between them. All individual lions, for example, are part of one group ego, as are all tigers or all pike.

The animals have their ego in the astral world.[14] It is as if someone stood behind a wall in which were ten holes, and pushed his ten fingers through. One would be unable to see him but could reasonably infer that the ten fingers all belonged to one hidden, motivating force. It is the same with the group ego. The individual animals are simply the limbs of what dwells in the astral world. These animal egos are different from the human 'I', although comparable from a spiritual point of view. An animal group ego is an extremely wise entity, far wiser than an individual human soul. Just think of certain species of bird, of the wisdom inherent in the height and direction of their flight, which allows them to leave winter behind them, and return in spring by a different route. We can recognize the wise influence of the group ego in their flight. The same wisdom can be found everywhere in the animal kingdom.

Human beings are very short-sighted and self-centred in their account of humanity's progress. In your schooldays you may well have learned about the innovations and impulses that shaped the modern world as it gradually emerged from the Middle Ages. Of course we must acknowledge the significant developments which arose at this time: the discovery of America, the invention of gunpowder and printing, and also of making paper. Of course it was a significant development when paper replaced the use of parchment. Yet the group soul of the wasps had already achieved this thousands of years before. The wasps' nest is made of the same kind of material as paper manufactured by human beings.

Only gradually will human beings come to discover that certain configurations of his spirit are connected with what the group souls have worked and woven into the world. These group souls are in continual movement. The clairvoyant can see a constant flickering along the length of the spine of animals; it is as if the spine is embedded in this dancing, flickering light. Innumerable currents of force that encircle the earth in all directions, somewhat like the trade winds, pulse through animals, flow around their spinal cord and influence them. The animal group souls pass in continual circulatory movement, at all heights and in all directions, around the earth. They are most wise, but they lack one thing: they know nothing of what we call love. Only in the human ego is love united with wisdom.

Each individual animal knows love in the form of sexual and parental love. In the animal, love is individualized, but the wisdom of the group ego is without love. The human being unites love and wisdom, whereas in the animal they are separate: the animal has love in its physical existence, and wisdom in the group ego's astral realm. We can learn an enormous amount by understanding such things.

But our modern, human ego only developed slowly. In former times we also had a group soul from which the individual soul gradually emerged...

As the human being evolved, the physical world grew more focused and sharply defined for him; but at the same time his powers of clairvoyant vision faded. The world of spirit became darker and dimmer as the physical world grew ever more defined and illumined ... The human being of ancient times descended into his physical body each morning and felt separate and single; but when he returned each night to the world of spirit he returned also to a unity and wholeness of which he was a part, a great company to which he belonged ...

Slowly individual consciousness developed out of this group soul. In accounts from the time of the Patriarchs we can find traces of the transition from the group soul to the individual soul. Before the time of Noah memory was of a quite different kind. Instead of being confined within the boundaries of a single life it reached back to encompass the lives of father, grandfather, great-grandfather and so on. In those of one blood, memory streamed back to long-gone generations.[15] Nowadays the authorities record the name of each individual, but in the days when people remembered what their father or grandfather had done a common name united all who shared the same blood and memory—such as 'Adam' or 'Noah'. These names did not refer to an individual life but to the stream of memory of whole groups and tribes, extending far beyond the lives of individual members ...

While we remained united with the group soul, as human beings, we were guided by higher powers. [But as this wanes] we are thrown back on our own resources. Then, if we do not find access to the necessary spiritual knowledge, we are in danger of becoming wholly isolated.

What can protect us from such spiritual isolation, from wandering aimlessly without the group soul's spiritual guidance? Let us be quite clear that the process of human individualization will become ever more apparent, and that in future people must increasingly relate to each other through their own free will. The old connections between people, based on blood, lineage and race, will soon be quite obsolete. Everything is tending towards the increasingly distinct individuality of human beings.

Yet the only possible way forward is, ultimately, one that leads back. Imagine a situation on earth in which human beings all wish to go their own way and find their own direction from within, becoming ever more distinct and sundered from each other. There would be a danger of fragmentation and isolation. Nowadays people are already wary of what might unify them spiritually. Today almost everyone has their own religion and considers their own opinion to be of paramount importance. Yet if people look inward, look closely at their ideals, they will find them to be in harmony with those of others. We can, for example, acknowledge that 3 times 3 equals 9; or that the three angles of a triangle add up to 180 degrees. These are matters of inner certainty about which we do not need to argue, and all spiritual truths, likewise, are of this kind. The science of the spirit teaches things which each person can discover for himself through his own inner effort. They lead him to complete agreement, peace and harmony with all others. If there are two conflicting opinions about a truth, then one of them must be mistaken. Our ideal must be to reach deeper and deeper within ourselves, for in doing so we find unity and peace.

To begin with there existed a human group soul. Gradually humanity emancipated itself from this. But as we continue to evolve we must have before us an ideal goal towards which we strive. When people are united in higher wisdom, when communities based on natural ties give way to ones arising through free will, a group soul descends once more from higher worlds. The aim of those at the forefront of our spiritual-scientific movement is for us to find through it a community in which human hearts can flow out towards the sources of wisdom, as plants reach out towards sunlight. Where separate egos are united by a common truth, the higher group soul can descend. If, together, we turn our hearts towards a higher wisdom, the group soul can anchor and embody itself in the environment we prepare for it. Earthly life will be enriched when human beings make it possible for spiritual beings to descend from higher worlds, which is the aim and ideal of spiritual science.

This living spiritual ideal was once revealed to humanity in a mighty and majestic form whose overwhelming power can show us how we can endeavour to help the unifying spirit incarnate amongst us through the unity of our souls. The event of Whitsun, in which a number of human beings met together with common purpose and were fired by a single feeling of the deepest love and devotion, stands before us as a great symbol and sign. The souls of these human beings were united in shock by the same shattering event. The unified stream of this one emotion enabled a higher entity, a uniting soul, to descend and reveal itself. This is made clear by the words which describe the coming of the Holy Spirit, the higher group soul, which divided itself and settled upon each individual in the form of fiery tongues. That is the great symbol and ideal for the future of humanity ...

Human beings must now try to create vessels in which the beings of higher worlds can pour themselves. The Easter event gave humanity the strength to internalize these mighty ideals and to strive for unity of spirit; the festival of Whitsun is the fruit born from the ripening of this strength.

The flowing of souls towards a unifying wisdom should continuously create a living connection with the powers and beings of higher worlds, and with the Whitsun festival itself, which people nowadays consider to be so unimportant. The science of the spirit will renew its significance for human beings. When people know what the descent of the Holy Spirit means for the future of humanity, new life will be breathed into the Whitsun festival. It will then no longer merely be a remembrance of the events in Jerusalem, but will become the ongoing festival of common soul endeavour. It will become the symbol and ideal of a future Whitsun fellowship, in which human beings will be joined together in truth, so that higher beings can incarnate among them. The extent to which the earth can fulfil itself in future, so that such ideals exert an influence in human life, depends on human beings themselves. If humanity endeavours to unite in this way with the truth, higher spirits will descend and unite with mankind.

8. One Fire, Many Tongues

Extract from a lecture given in Dornach on
9 May 1923

'Speaking in tongues' at Whitsun is in many ways a reversal of the biblical story of Babel, when a once unified humanity was sundered. The 'babble' of many languages is reforged into heartfelt understanding above and beyond all human differences.

The disciples no longer saw him after 40 days because their vision lost its power. They then said: 'Now he has gone away from us.' The Ascension was an event that did, of course, make the disciples feel very sad. They said: 'Although he died, although his enemies crucified him, he dwelt among us for 40 days. Now he is no longer among us, but has returned to the wide expanse of the cosmos.'

And they felt truly downcast. Not the usual kind of sadness, but something profound. And the ten days of which we then read, those ten days were a time when the disciples and apostles turned inwards, looking deep into their hearts, using their inner strength to think of all the things the Christ had said to them. Those ten days were enough for them to be able to say afterwards: 'Yes, we too can know all this. This wisdom also lives in us.' And now, after ten days, they felt strong enough also to teach the wisdom to others. The tongues of fire, which is an image of this, descended upon their heads. That was the Pentecost thought, embodied in the tongues of fire. In their great sadness, having pondered all their experiences, unable to see the Christ any longer, they were able to turn inwards in such a way that they themselves could begin to teach.

And we read the beautiful words that they then began to 'speak in tongues'. But here we have to understand a little how people expressed things in those earlier times. You should not, of course, imagine that the apostles started to speak Chinese or Japanese or German. What is meant, in the way such things were expressed at that time, is that all they had weighed in their thoughts in the ten days between Ascension and Pentecost had given them great tolerance and understanding. Now they no longer accentuated the differences between religions but spoke of one religion uniting all human beings. That is what is meant by saying they were able to speak in all tongues: they spoke of one religion uniting humanity.

And that is the best of all thoughts for Pentecost—one religion for all humanity. You see, the greatest harm has always come to humanity from fanaticism in religious matters, from exclusivity, with Christianity opposed to Buddhism, Judaism and all other religions ...

The divine spirit we should venerate is not attached to a particular place on earth, but is connected with the power of the sun, the living nature of the sun which Christ has absorbed. And the sun is truly for all humanity. No one in Europe can say that the sun shining on his head is a different sun from the one enjoyed by Egyptians, or Chinese or Australians. Anyone who truly accepts that the Christ power comes from the all-present sun has to accept the overarching religion that belongs to all humanity ...

The disciples recognized fully that the sun religion had come. They were able to 'speak in tongues', which means they spoke of a religion of reconciliation, of tolerance for all humanity. That is the Pentecost idea; but as you know, this has not yet come to fulfilment. Yet it must come to fulfilment. It must be truly understood that the Christ brought something to this earth that does not depend on any particular doctrine or teaching, but is based on a universal fact ...

9. Warmth Transmutes Matter

Extract from a lecture given in Dornach on
16 May 1920

While this excerpt makes no direct reference to Whitsun it relates to it in two ways.

Firstly in the reversal of direction which Whitsun embodies – from receiving gifts from without to internalizing, individualizing and pouring them out again in transformed, self-directed activity. Parzival, whose name indicates perseverance and penetration of matter, is a figure who represents courage, endurance and ever-increasing spiritual perception.

Secondly Steiner reiterates a theme, which often surfaces in this volume, of imaginative pictures and thinking that have a germinal power and can give us an enhanced connection to reality, or empty pictures that remain a mere shadow of earthly existence. The Son reverses human decline and dissolution, and as such is a seed force for humanity. Seeds of course, as they ripen, have a close connection with heat and warmth, and Steiner here touches on warmth as a moral reality uniting human beings.

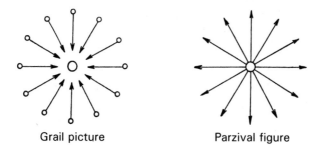

Grail picture   Parzival figure

When we live in pictures we really *are not.* When we live in mere thoughts it is the surest sign we do not exist in a substantial sense. Thoughts must be filled with substantiality. So that the human being would not continue to live in mere pictures, so that inner substantiality might once more exist in human beings, [Christ] entered through the Mystery of Golgotha . . . This central force was now to give back to the human soul reality, which had become mere picture. However, this was not immediately understood. In the Middle Ages we have the last echoes of this in the twelve around King Arthur's round table. But this was soon replaced by something else, the Parzival legend, which contrasts one man with the twelve—one man who develops twelvefoldness out of his own inner core. Thus in contrast to the first picture [see above, left], which was essentially the Grail picture, must be set the Parzival picture [see above, right], in which what the human being possesses within him rays out from the centre.

The endeavour of those in the Middle Ages who wished to understand Parzival, who wished to make the Parzival striving active in the human soul, was to introduce true substantiality, real inner being into the image life that could crystallize out in the human being after all materiality had filtered away. Whereas the Grail legend still embodies an in-streaming direction from without, the Parzival figure is now set against this, raying out from the centre, into mere pictures, the inner life that can restore reality to them.

The Parzival legend thus represented the striving of humanity in the Middle Ages to find the way to Christ within. It represents an instinctive striving to understand what lives as the Christ in the evolution of humanity. If one studies inwardly what was experienced in this figure of Parzival, and compares it with the content of creeds and faiths, one can receive a strong impulse towards what needs to happen today. People are now satisfied with the mere husk of the word 'Christ', believing that they thus possess Christ, whereas even theologians do not possess him, but remain at the level of more superficial, external interpretation and exegesis. In the Middle Ages there was still so much direct consciousness left of such things that by comprehending the representative of humanity, Parzival, people were able to wrest their way upwards to the figure of Christ. If we reflect on this we also gain an impression of the human being's place in the whole universe. Throughout the natural world, the conversion and transmutation of forces and energy prevails. Only in the human being is matter cast out by pure thought. The matter cast out of the human being by pure thought is actually annihilated, and passes into nothingness. In the human being, therefore, a place exists in the universe where matter ceases to exist.

If we reflect on this, we must think of all earth existence as follows. Here is the earth, and on the earth the human being, into whom matter passes. Everywhere else matter is transmuted, transformed, but in the human being it is annihilated. The material earth will pass away as matter is gradually transformed by the human being. When, some day, all the substance of the earth has passed through the human organism, being used there for thinking, the earth will cease to be a planetary body. And what the human being will have gained from this earth existence will be pictures. These however will have a new reality, will preserve a primal reality. This reality is the one proceeding from the core force which entered human evolution through the Mystery of Golgotha. Looking towards the end of our earth, therefore, what do we see? The earth will end when all its substance is destroyed, as described above. The human being will then possess pictures of all that has taken place during Earth evolution. At the end of Earth evolution the earth would, without the Mystery of Golgotha, have been absorbed back into the universe and remain merely pictures without reality. What makes them real, however, is the fact of the Mystery of Golgotha in human evolution, giving these pictures inner reality for future life. Through the Mystery of Golgotha a new beginning becomes possible for the earth's future existence . . .

We have not grasped Christianity until we can say to ourselves: precisely in the domain of heat a change is taking place in the human being that results in matter being destroyed and a purely picture existence arising out of matter . . . We do not participate only in the evolving material universe, but in its decay too, and we are now in the process of raising ourselves out of it to mere picture existence and then permeating ourselves with what we can only devote ourselves to in free will—the Christ being. For he stands in human evolution in a way that means our connection with him can only be a free one. Anyone who is *compelled* to acknowledge Christ cannot find his kingdom. He can only come to the universal Father God who, however, in our world now only participates in a decaying world, and precisely on account of this decay has sent the Son ...

The phantom which external science nowadays presents as the human being, that illusory picture which shows us to be a mere configuration of mineral substance, simply does not exist. The human being is just as much a fluid as a solid organism. He is also an air organism and, above all, one of heat. When we reach the level of heat we find the transition from space to time; and the element of soul flows in the temporal. Through heat we pass more and more from space into time, and it becomes possible to seek the moral in the physical. People with short-sighted views will scarcely grasp the connection of the moral with the physical in human nature—for one can certainly live as a miscreant without any apparent physical repercussions, remaining a properly formed human being. Yet no one thinks of examining the heat condition of such a person, which is changed in far subtler ways than people imagine, and affects what a person carries with him through death. Today people generally look upwards into abstraction and down into the physical, material realm. But we do not find the transitionary sphere unless we recognize the inwardly stirring heat or warmth lying between these, which has, at least for human sensibility, a physical as well as a soul aspect. We can develop warmth for our fellows morally—soul warmth as the counterpart of physical warmth ... Why do we speak of 'warm' feelings'? Because we feel, we experience, that the feeling we call 'warm' is an image of outer physical warmth. Warmth percolates into the image. And what is only soul warmth today will in a future cosmic existence play a physical part, for the Christ impulse will live within it. What today is simply picture warmth in our world of feeling will, when earthly warmth has disappeared, live, become physical in Christ substance, Christ nature. Let us try to find that delicate connection between external physical warmth and what we instinctively call warmth of feeling; let us try to find it ...

10. The Spirit Lives in Time

Extract from a lecture given in Dornach on
4 June 1924

Like empty pictures contrasted with living imagination,
Steiner here distinguishes between earthly, spatial con-
cepts and what he calls 'time', which here refers to a
continuous, unbroken time experience, or eternity. What
we usually call 'time' is our spatialized concept of it:
separate succeeding events measured by spatial changes.

We normally regard our entry into the spatial world as
birth, and our departure from it as death. But in the three
Rose Cross meditations – Ex deo nascimur, In Christo
morimur, and Per spiritum sanctum reviviscimus
(Out of God we are born, In Christ we die, Through the
Holy Spirit we live again) – we move from Christmas
through Easter to Whitsun and discover, in Christ, that
death is merely a door that opens into new life in the
spirit.

We can only look up to the sun in the right way
(even if only in our mind) when we forget space
and consider time alone. The sun does not only

radiate light, but radiates space itself; and in looking at the sun we are gazing into a realm beyond
space. The sun is the unique star that it is because
we gaze through it into a world beyond space. And
from that world Christ came to humanity ... and
brought the element of time; and when the human
heart, soul and spirit unite with Christ, we can
again receive the stream of time that flows through
all eternity. What else can we human beings do
when we die — when, in other words, we leave the
realm of space — than hold fast to him who gives us
back time again? By the Mystery of Golgotha the
human being had become to so great an extent a
being of space that time was lost to him. Christ gave
time back again to human beings.

If then, in going forth from the world of space,
people are not to die in their souls as well as their
bodies, they must die in Christ ... Since the Mystery
of Golgotha we cannot conceive of death, the
boundary of our earthly life, without this thought:
'We must die in Christ.'

Physical science speaks of a movement of the sun;
and it can do so, for within the spatial picture of the
cosmos which surrounds us we perceive by certain
phenomena that the sun is in movement. But this is
in fact only a reflection of the sun's movement
projected into the realm of space. If we are speaking
of the real sun it is nonsense to say that it moves in

space, for space itself is poured out by the sun. The sun not only radiates light, it also creates the realm of space. And the movement of the sun is only a spatial one within space. Outside of space it is a movement in time ...

To his intimate disciples Christ spoke these words: 'Behold the life of the earth: it is related to the life of the cosmos. When you look out on the earth and the surrounding cosmos it is the Father whose life permeates this universe. The Father God is the God of space. But I tell you that I have come from the sun, from time — the time that receives you only when you die. I have brought you myself from the realm of time. If you receive me you receive time and will not be held spellbound in space ...

Let us now imagine a human soul who closes himself off entirely within earthly existence. He can still sense the divine, for he is born from it: *Ex deo nascimur.* Then let us imagine that he no longer merely encloses himself within the world of space but receives the Christ who came from the world of time into the world of space, who brought time itself into the world of earthly space. At death the soul will then overcome death. *Ex deo nascimur. In Christo morimur.* But Christ himself brings the message that when space is overcome and one has learned to recognize the sun as the creator of space, when one feels oneself placed through Christ into the sun, lifted into the living sun, then the earthly and physical vanishes and only the etheric and astral are there.[16] Then the etheric comes to life, no longer as the blue expanse of the sky but as the crimson-red gleaming radiance of the cosmos; and from this reddish light the stars no longer twinkle down upon us but gently touch us with their loving influence.

If we really enter into all this we can experience ourselves standing upon the earth, but the physical has been put aside. The etheric is still with us though, streaming through and out of us in the crimson light. The stars are then no longer points of light but emanations of love, like the caressing hand of a human being. As we feel all this—the divine within ourselves, the divine cosmic fire flaming forth from within us as our very being, ourselves within the etheric world, the spirit's living expression in the astral radiance pouring through the cosmos—then there comes to life within us the inner experience of spirit radiance which is the human being's high calling in the universe.

When those to whom Christ revealed these things had let the revelation sink deeply enough into their being, its effect became manifest for them in the fiery tongues of the Pentecost. At first they experienced the falling away, the discarding of the earthly and physical as death. But then they felt: 'This is not death. In place of the physical nature of earth there now dawns upon us instead the spirit selfhood of the universe.[17] *Per spiritum sanctum reviviscimus ...*

The language of the stars speaks to us through the three thoughts of Christmas, Easter and Whitsun: through the Christmas thought inasmuch as the earth is a planetary star embedded in the whole cosmos; through the Easter thought inasmuch as the most radiant of stars, the sun, gives us its gifts of grace; and through the Whitsun thought inasmuch as what lies hidden beyond the stars shines into the soul, and shines forth from the soul in the fiery tongues of Pentecost ...

HUMAN FREEDOM AND
THE WORD

11. The Lost Word

Extract from a lecture given in Berlin on Whit
Monday, 5 June 1905

*Only human beings speak in words and have freedom of
choice about their actions. This dual capacity in us, which
is the spark of spirit, needs to resonate again with the
universal flame of spirit it once separated from. Then our
words can reconnect with the power of the Word.*

Among the allegories and symbols we wished to
discuss in these lectures there is also the symbol of
the so-called Lost Word which is to be found
again...

Pentecost is connected with that perception of
our inmost being which was present in early
Christianity but which Christianity has gradually
lost in the various western Churches. Pentecost is
the festival which every year should freshly remind
human beings of their liberation — of what we can
call the freedom of the human soul.

How did the human being really come to what
we call his freedom, that is to say his ability to

distinguish between good and evil, and to do either good or evil? You know that the human being has passed through a long sequence of evolution before arriving at the stage where he stands today, and that we have passed the mid-point of this evolution. The mid-point of the whole of evolution lies roughly in the middle of the Atlantean period which preceded our own epoch.[18]

... What we human beings did not possess before the mid-point of our Earth evolution was freedom of choice between good and evil. We cannot talk about good and evil in the lower kingdoms of nature. It would be ridiculous to debate whether a mineral wished to crystallize or not, for it does so if the appropriate conditions are present. It would be equally ridiculous to ask whether the lily wants to blossom, or to ask the lion to abstain voluntarily from killing and devouring other animals. Only with the human being, at our current stage of evolution, can we speak about 'freedom of choice'. Only to human beings do we ascribe the capacity to distinguish between good and evil. In the great symbol of the Fall the Bible describes how the human being gained this capacity — in the scene of the temptation where the devil or Lucifer appears to Eve and persuades her to eat from the Tree of Knowledge. As a result the human being gained free will, and thus embarked on the second part of his evolutionary path. Prior to that evolutionary mid-point we can no more enquire into freedom, into the human being's capacity for good and evil, than we can do so today for minerals, plants and animals ...

Spirit, Son and Father are as though entombed in the earth: the Father in the physical body, the Son in the etheric body and the Spirit in the astral body.[19] However, the human being has developed his ego[20] and has become self-aware. Now he must learn to work right down into the physical. That will develop in the future. At present he is working into his astral body, the symbol for which is the descent of the Holy Spirit into those who are to become leaders and exemplars for humanity. What has taken up this Spirit is something within us which is akin to it.

Before the Son could become effective ... a part of the universal principle of spirit had to break away, be thrust down, and wander other paths. This is expressed in the serpent, the symbol of knowledge and the luciferic principle.[21] It was this spark of spirit which made us into free beings and enabled us to desire what is good out of our own impulse. The Spirit which descended to human beings at the great festival of Whitsun is akin to the spirit which was thrust down, and which is embodied in the figure of Prometheus. This has blown the spark into a flame, so that our ego can make up its mind to follow the Spirit, just as it will later follow the Son, and still later the Father. The human being certainly developed the capacity for evil, but on the other hand this was the price of being guided back to the world of the gods from which he originated. That is the connection between Pentecost and the luciferic principle. Thus the Whitsun festival is also the festival of Prometheus and freedom ...

The Word became entombed in the earth ... The human being will raise this Word from the dead, out of the earth; but first the spirit must live in him to enable the Word to resonate within him. This was attained by the apostles at Pentecost. In *Light on the Path* we find the words:[22] 'Acquire knowledge and you will have speech.' Speech comes with true knowledge, which descends like the tongues of fire on the apostles at holy Pentecost. When the inner Word, which is akin to the divine cosmic Word, descends into everything etheric, imbuing it with vitality, then the human being will no longer speak out of himself alone but out of the divine spirit. He is then the messenger of the Godhead and proclaims its inner Word out of his own free will.

Thus did the inner Word become alive in the apostles, spreading its influence outwards from them. They proclaimed the fiery Word and were aware of their role as messengers of the Godhead.

Therefore the Holy Spirit hovers over them in the form of fiery tongues. They prepare humanity to receive the Logos ... Once this has happened the Christ principle will be drawn into humanity. This is what the initiates too had in mind when they said, somewhat like Heraclitus: 'If, in escaping from the earthly, you ascend to the free ether with faith in immortality, you become an immortal spirit free of death and of the physical ...

We best celebrate Pentecost by realizing what deep truths wisdom has implanted into this festival. To celebrate a festival really means to unite oneself in spirit with the cosmic Spirit.

12. From Empty Phrase to Living Word

Extract from a lecture given in Stuttgart on
8 June 1919

*In this fiery, and in some places furious excerpt, largely
relating to the malaise in the education system, Steiner
rails against empty words and meaningless phrase-
mongering. The spirit in words is what is important, not
their empty husks, which contain no impetus for real
change or action.*

A great deal is being said these days about the
unimportance of the Word, and that 'in the beginning was the Deed'. My dear friends, an age like
ours will even find a false use for the Gospel. Word
has become mere chattered phrase and the deed
thoughtless brutality. An age like ours turns away
from the Word with good reason, because it can
only find in it mere phrase; and the deed that it
knows becomes thoughtless brutality ...

We must fill our souls with what can really
inspire us when we speak. We must find a way to
make the heart speak through the lips. We must

find a way to penetrate our words with our entire being. Otherwise the word seduces us, tempts us with illusion, lures us away from reality's gravity. We must put away forever the attitude which lures us to church to be elevated there from life's earnestness, and to hear gratifying phrases such as that the Lord will make everything well, will deliver us from our evils. We must look within ourselves, within our own souls, for forces which are divine forces, which have been implanted in us during the world's evolution for us to use, so that we can receive God into our individual souls. We should not hearken to preaching about some external God – which allows our souls to lie in indolent repose on philistine sofas, of which we are so fond whenever spiritual life is at stake ...

The 'spirit of law' which our age still worships today was right for the Romans. For what was this spirit of law? A deep meaning lies hidden in the legend of Rome's origins.[23] Brutes were held together in order to combat the worst animal-human instincts. That is what Roman laws were for, to herd wild animals together. But we should realize that we have become human beings, and should not worship the spirit of law which arose from a legitimate Roman instinct to tame brutish human passions. The Roman spirit that still prevails today in our legalistic structures is universally intended to restrain wild human passions and prevent them from being unleashed ...

As to the spirit of Whitsun today, one can hardly say that if it were not cherished and cultivated it would find much fertile ground on which to fall. There is plenty of opportunity to see how this Whitsun spirit is misunderstood on all sides ... People do not want to have to think; they prefer ... to utter beautiful phrases and do not want their thoughts to become deeds. And anyone who takes their phrases seriously is violently attacked ...

The unreal phrase is the religious chatter of the world; the brutal, unspiritual act is militarism, the fundamental evil of our time. Until one realizes how thoroughly these two things are ingrained in our perverted educational life, one cannot think fruitfully about what needs to be done. Everything else is simply a quack remedy.

What must be done, my friends, must be based fully on reality, which bears spirit within it. Denial of the spirit, on the other hand, renders everything absurd ...

When one says today that humanity must learn to think in new ways, people believe at most that one is using the same phrase as they themselves use — and they immediately translate it into mere phrases and utopias. But it makes a difference, surely, whether some popular orator says that mankind must 'learn new lessons' or whether this is said by someone who knows that humanity's habits of artificial and shallow thinking have created such depths of false thoughts that these reach down into the very structure of the human nervous system ... Anyone unable to distinguish between phrase and reality can refer you, for instance, to the editorial of today's local paper and say: 'Look, someone else is also preaching about a "new beginning for humanity".' But it is not a question of comparing words, for then we fall into word idolatry. Today we need to see reality, and protect ourselves from succumbing to mere word worship ... The Pentecost festival should pour out on human souls an admonition to scorn mere phrases and re-engage with reality. In the fields of science, art, religion — in fact wherever you turn — people talk in phrases that stick in the throat and do not encompass the whole human reality ...

We need to combat the love of illusion that is so widespread today. Many feel comfortable when they can delude themselves about reality. Instead of Christ in me, who arouses my strength, who liberates powerful forces within me, they profess the Christ who is external to them, and who mercifully frees them from sins without them having to lift a finger or draw on their own forces ...

Especially if one wants to move on to the true

Pentecost spirit, from babbling words to seed-bearing words, then one must repeatedly and earnestly examine one's own habitual concepts in order to see what it is that one does not want to make really new concepts for, what it is that we can chatter about without understanding while still clinging to old concepts ...

The modern economic order has harnessed the proletariat to factories and capitalism, but it is easier for these people to understand the real needs of the time than for the middle classes who cling so tenaciously to their positions, income and pensions, and do not want to think. When a movement arises which rejects phrase-mongering and chatter, which instead offers seed-thoughts for action,[24] people cannot accept it as anything other than mere phrase ... Today of course the economic pressures which exist are the cause of frightful eruptions in the social organism. But is this now to be succeeded by jostling for position and the worst kind of bureaucracy? Do people who have now (although a little late) finally learned that they can no longer depend on 'throne and altar' actually believe that it would be any safer to depend in the same way on the state treasury and the state budget? Capitalism has succeeded in gradually changing respect for the altar into respect for hard cash. Pseudo-socialism will likewise know how to change pseudo-respect for power that no longer exists, but lives on in empty phrase, into corporate idolatry and corporate hierarchy.

What humanity needs today for a renewal of the spirit is the courage to realize that humanity's life of spirit has become religious chatter on the one hand and thoughtless, brutal militarism on the other. Today's typical citizen in this modern capitalist age feels most comfortable when engaged in counting his personal pension, averting his eyes as he does so from the realities thus created. On the one hand the Gospel becomes mere chatter about love of one's neighbour and brotherly feelings, while on the other a person sits there cutting out his pension coupons, simultaneously cutting such brotherly love to pieces with his scissors ...

When celebrating Whitsun, these are the things that must be said today in relation to the need to renew education and schools. The unctuous talk you hear everywhere has no place. People need to hearken to words that arise from today's realities. Then it will be possible for the real Pentecost spirit to descend among us, for little tongues of fire to extend into all that will arise in future from liberated life of the spirit ... so that in future the emancipated spirit, which is the real Holy Spirit, can further humanity's spiritual evolution.

These words may be ones that today's religious

chatterers will not exactly regard as 'Christian'. But humanity will have to decide whether the Christian talk of contemporary people originates in the spirit in which Peter denied his Lord three times, or whether it arises from the spirit that said: 'I am with you until the end of time.' Those who today can hear only the spirit of the past, even in Christianity, will be the phrase-makers and chatterers. Those who receive the living spirit today, and make it real in the transformation and renewal of society, will be those in whom one may be able to see the true Christ dawning.

13. 'The Truth Shall Set You Free'

Extract from a lecture given in Hamburg on Whit
Sunday, 15 May 1910

*In a sweeping vista of humanity's evolutionary future
Steiner here draws together all the threads of other lectures in this volume to emphasize that Whitsun is the
festival of the ever-renewed Word, of the living spirit
connecting each person with all others. When we speak,
our words are of course borne on the breath; and the
'rushing mighty wind' of Whitsun is a reminder of a
dynamic, unifying force in the atmosphere we all share,
and of the Word which, if we receive it, can live in our
individual words.*

Festivals are beacons of remembrance, turning our
thoughts and feelings to the past. Their meaning
awakens in us thoughts that link us to all that our
souls held holy in distance ages. But thoughts of
humanity's future (that is, the future of our own
soul) are also roused in us when we understand the
content of these festivals. Feelings of enthusiasm for
the future are awakened in us, ideals inspire our

will — which gives us the strength to undertake future tasks in an ever more fulfilling way.

To best understand the Whitsun festival, let us therefore turn our gaze both backwards to the past and forwards to the future. Its deep significance for western humanity can be apparent to us through the mighty picture we all know well, which speaks to the very depths of the soul. Having fulfilled the Mystery of Golgotha, the inaugurator and initiator of Christianity dwelt for a time among those able to perceive him, in the embodiment which he then assumed. The events that followed are presented to us in a significant series of images. In a mighty vision, known as the Ascension, his closest disciples beheld the dispersal of that bodily form which he had assumed after the Mystery of Golgotha. Then, ten days later, there followed what is expressed for us in another picture, which speaks powerfully to all hearts with the will to understand it. The disciples of Christ, those who were the first to understand him, are gathered together. Deep in their hearts they feel the mighty impulse that has entered human evolution through him. Gathered together in deepest devotion on the day of Pentecost, the time-honoured festival of their people, they wait expectantly for the promised events to be fulfilled in their souls. What is described as the 'rushing mighty wind' lifts their souls up into higher vision.

They are summoned to turn their gaze on what is yet to come to pass, on what will await them when, with the fire impulse they have received into their hearts, they live on earth in future incarnation after incarnation.

Next the soul is presented with the picture of the 'tongues of fire' which descend upon the head of each of the disciples. Another tremendous vision here reveals to them the future of this impulse. Gathered together, and beholding in spirit the world of spirit, these people, the first to understand Christ, feel as if they were not speaking to people near to them in geographical space or close to them in time; instead they feel their hearts borne far, far away, amongst the many different peoples and nations of the globe. They feel as if something lives in their hearts which is translatable into all languages, which human hearts will be able to understand. In this mighty vision of the future of Christianity which rises before them, these first disciples feel themselves as though surrounded by future disciples amongst all the earth's people. They feel as if they will, one day, have the power to proclaim the Gospel in words understandable not only to those directly near them in space and time, but to all they encounter who will live on earth in future times. This was the inner content of soul and feeling of these earliest disciples of Christ, at the first Christian festival of Whitsun.

Let us now consider the interpretation of these pictures in their deepest esoteric Christian meaning. The spirit, also rightly named the Holy Spirit, sent its forces down to the earth in the first descent to earth of Christ Jesus. It next manifested when Jesus was baptized by John the Baptist. Then, once again, this same spirit, in another form, that of many single, shining, fiery tongues, descended upon each single one of the first Christian disciples.

We are told about this Holy Spirit at the Whitsun festival in a quite special way, but we must get clear in our minds the meaning of the words 'Holy Spirit' as they are used in the Gospels ...

Through the Christ impulse a new conception came about ... replacing the common folk spirit of a people with one which, though certainly related to it, worked at a far higher level. Connected to the whole of mankind, as the earlier spirit had been connected to a particular nation or people, this spirit was to imbue the human being with the power to say: 'I no longer feel I belong only to a part of humanity but to the whole of it. I am part of all mankind and will become ever more part of it.' This force, through which a universal human quality streamed into the whole of mankind, was ascribed to the Holy Spirit. Thus the spirit which expressed itself in inheritance, in the force flowing through the mother, was raised up to Holy Spirit.

We may therefore now understand that the power of the Holy Spirit is what will raise each person ever more beyond all that differentiates and separates him from others, so that he becomes a member, beyond nationality, of the whole of humanity on earth. This is a power that works as a bond of soul between each and every individual, no matter what body or racial characteristic they possess...

At the baptism by John the spirit stands before us in the image of the dove. Now, however, another picture appears — that of the fiery tongues. It is as a single dove, a single form, that the Holy Spirit manifests at the baptism by John; but it manifests as many single tongues at the Whitsun event. And each of these single tongues of fire brings inspiration to an individual, to each of the individuals who were Christianity's first disciples.

What meaning does this symbol of Whitsun have for our souls? After Christ, the bearer of the universal human spirit, had completed his work on earth, after he had allowed all sheaths of his earthly embodiment to disperse and enter, whole and unified, into the spiritual essence of the earth, only then could those who understood the Christ impulse receive into their hearts the possibility of speaking of it, of being active in its service. The outer, earthly manifestation of the Christ impulse vanished at Ascension into the single totality of the world of spirit; then ten days later it emerged again from each single, individual heart of its first followers. And because the same spirit that had worked in the power of the Christ impulse now reappeared in multiple form, the first disciples of Christianity became the bearers and preachers of the Christ message.

This event at the beginning of Christian history is a mighty beacon and sign to us. It reminds us that just as each single one of the first disciples received the Christ impulse into themselves, just as it was granted to them to receive it in the form of tongues of fire, as inspiration in their souls, so all of us can, when we strive to understand the Christ impulse, receive its power individualized into our own hearts, can become ever more imbued by it and receive the strength which enables us to serve it ever more fully. The more we perfect ourselves the more we can feel that the Holy Spirit speaks out of our own inner being. The Holy Spirit can increasingly penetrate our thinking, feeling and will, becoming also an individual spirit in each single human individual in which it works.

This Holy Spirit enables us to evolve as human beings, to become free human souls. As the spirit of freedom it streamed out through the first disciples of Christianity at the first Whitsun. It is the spirit whose most significant characteristic is indicated by Christ himself when he says: 'You shall know the truth, and the truth shall set you free.' We can become free only in the spirit. So long as we cling to the physical nature in which our spirit dwells, we remain its slave. We can become free only when we rediscover ourselves in spirit, and through the spirit gain mastery over what is within us. Our true spirit is the universal human spirit which we recognize as the Pentecostal power of the Holy Spirit entering us, which we must bring to birth within us and allow to be revealed.

Thus the Whitsun symbol is transformed for us into the most powerful of human ideals, the development of the human soul into a self-enclosed yet free individual ...

When we feel inwardly that we can raise ourselves above ourselves, we can then strive to make this real. We shall then have the will to liberate our inner being, to pull it clear as it were from its bondage to our outer nature. Of course we still dwell in our external self, but at the same time we become fully conscious of inner spiritual power. This moment at which, in this inner Easter festival of the soul, we grow aware that we can free ourselves, also determines whether we move on to attain the

Whitsun festival, whether we may fill the spirit that has discovered itself within itself with a content that is not of this but the spiritual world. This spiritual content alone can make us free. It is the spiritual truth of which Christ said: 'You shall know the truth, and the truth shall set you free' ...

The Christ impulse is an impulse of freedom. Its true effect does not reveal itself when it is active outside the human soul but only within the individual human soul itself. So it was that those who first understood the Christ felt themselves called through the Whitsun event to proclaim what now lived in their own souls; what, in the revelation and inspiration of their own souls, revealed itself to them as the content of Christ's teaching. They were aware that the Christ impulse had worked in the holy preparation which they underwent before the Whitsun festival; they felt themselves called through the power of the Christ impulse working within them to let speak the fiery tongues, the individualized Holy Spirit within them, and to go forth to proclaim the Gospel of Christ. It was not simply the words Christ had once spoken to them that those first disciples recognized as words of Christ. They recognized as Christ's words all that arises through the power of a soul that feels the Christ impulse within itself. To this end did the Holy Spirit pour itself in individualized form into each single human soul, so that each one might develop the power to feel the Christ impulse within him. For such a soul Christ's words gain new force and meaning when he says: 'I am with you always, even unto the end of the world.'

Those therefore who earnestly desire to experience the Christ impulse may also feel called upon, by what the Christ impulse arouses in their hearts, to proclaim the Word of Christ afresh, however new and different it may sound in each succeeding epoch. The Holy Spirit was not poured down so that we might cling to the few words of the Gospels spoken in the first decade of Christianity, but so the Gospel of Christ may continually speak anew to us. As human souls progress from epoch to epoch, from incarnation to incarnation, they need new things to be spoken to them. Should our souls, advancing from incarnation to incarnation, hear always only the Gospel words spoken when they were incarnated in bodies at the time Christ appeared on earth in physical embodiment? The Christ impulse contains the power to speak to all, until the end of earth's cycle of time. For this to be, however, the message of Christ must resound to ever-advancing human souls in a way appropriate to them in each new age. So when we feel the full strength and power of the Whitsun impulse, we should also feel that it is our task to attend to

Christ's words: 'I am with you always, even to the end of earth's cycle of time.' And when you fill yourselves with the Christ impulse you can hear the Word, which came through Christ at the founding of Christianity, resounding on through all ages — the Word which Christ speaks to all future times because he is with us forever, the Word which all can hear who have the will to hear it ...

Christ came down to earth because the power of the deed on Golgotha had to work upon human beings dwelling in physical bodies. Hence the Christ power can only work, initially, on those who are incarnated in a physical body. When, in our earthly life, we have received insight into the power of the Mystery of Golgotha, this impulse can then continue to work and perfect itself in us after death. Only as much of it as we have absorbed between birth and death can mature in us, however. We need to return to earth again to perfect it further. Only in successive earthly lives can we learn to understand all that lives in the Christ impulse. We could never understand it if we lived only once on earth. This impulse, therefore, must lead us through repeated earth lives because the earth is the place for the discovery of the meaning of the Mystery of Golgotha.

And so Christianity is only complete if we replace the assumption that we could fulfil the Christ impulse and ideal in one life by the other thought, that this can happen only through repeated earth lives. What we experience of it on earth we can then bring back into the spiritual world. We can bring back as much as we have grasped on earth of the Christ impulse, which—as the most significant impulse for all earthly life—had to be accomplished on the earth. We can see then that the thought which spiritual revelation adds to Christianity is one born out of Christianity itself, that of reincarnation. When we understand this we will realize the significance for us of the Whitsun revelation as gained through spiritual science. Such awareness assures us that we can experience a renewal of the revelation of the power of the 'fiery tongues' that descended upon those who first understood the Christ ...

Before the close of this century, new forces will develop in the human soul which will lead to the unfolding of a kind of etheric clairvoyance. This will allow, as if through natural development, a renewal for certain human beings of the event that Paul experienced at Damascus. For the human being's heightened spiritual faculties, Christ will return in an etheric[25] garb. Increasing numbers of souls will share in what Paul experienced at Damascus. Then it will become apparent in the world that the science of the spirit heralds a renewed and transformed truth of the Christ impulse. Only those people will understand the new revelation who believe that the fresh stream of the life of spirit into which Christ once and for all times poured himself will remain a living source for all future ages. Whoever does not wish to believe this may choose to preach an outmoded form of Christianity. But whoever believes in the Whitsun event and understands it will also become aware that the original Christian gospel will never cease evolving, will continue to speak to humanity in ever new ways; that the individualized soul worlds of the Holy Spirit, of the tongues of fire, will always remain present, and that in ever-renewed fire and impetus the human soul will be able to live with and live out of the Christ impulse.

We can believe in Christianity's future when we truly understand the Whitsun thought. Its mighty picture then comes before us with a force that works like one present in the soul itself. Then we can feel the future as the first disciples felt it when the Holy Spirit inspired them — if only we are willing to bring to life in our souls something which overleaps all boundaries dividing humanity, which speaks a language that all souls, all the world over, can understand. We can experience the power of peace, love and harmony which lies in the Whitsun thought. And we can feel this Whitsun thought enlivening our Whitsun festival. We can feel it as an assurance of our hope for freedom and eternity. Because we feel the individualized spirit awakening in our souls, there awakens in us its most significant attribute: unending life of the spirit. By sharing in the spirit we can become conscious of our immortality, our eternal existence. And in the Whitsun thought we truly realize the power of those primal words passed on by initiate after initiate, which reveal to us the meaning of wisdom and eternity. Handed on from epoch to epoch, these words reveal the Whitsun thought to us. Today, for the first time, they can resound openly and unrestrictedly, so that all humanity can grasp and share in them:

> Being weaves with being in breadths of space,
> being follows being through cycles of time.
> If, O human being, you remain
> in breadths of space, in cycles of time, you dwell
> in transience alone.
> But when, divining or knowing, your soul can
>   gaze
> upon eternity, then mightily
> it lifts itself beyond all space and time.

Afterword

Robert Frost's poem 'The Tuft of Flowers'[26] is a strangely quiet yet atmospheric work, somehow tense with a creative pressure which the poem's vessel contains but never allows to spill over and dissipate. It is full of a presence which is also absence, of a silent figure who does not appear in the flesh but imbues the poem with a sense of invisible companionship. This poem, I think, strikes many resonances with Whitsun.

Frost first describes himself going to turn the hay. He is following in the steps of the mower who had cut the grass in the dewy dawn, before the sun rose. He listens for the sounds of the whetstone, but the mower has gone, and this engenders in him a feeling of loneliness. But even as he silently concedes the isolation of all human beings, reminiscent perhaps of the loneliness of the disciples after Ascension, a 'bewildered butterfly'—a metaphor of his own wandering, questing spirit—passes by, looking for the flowers that used to stand there and have now been cut down. The gifts that once grew naturally have withered, but the mower has not razed everything. His scythe has spared a 'leaping tongue of bloom'. Here the poem beautifully articulates the mysterious mower's love of the earth and his 'sheer morning gladness'. There is a quickening of joy, a feeling of the poem's resurrection as the mower almost becomes one with the dawn and the sun itself, his 'long scythe whispering to the ground' in ethereal communication with the earth.

Out of the poet's sense of loneliness, then—of having to be, as the mower had been, alone—a sudden sense of spirit kinship is kindled, so that, as Frost writes: 'Henceforth I worked no more alone; / But glad with him, I worked as with his aid . . . / And dreaming, as it were, held brotherly speech / With one whose thought I had not hoped to reach.'

As far as I know the figure of Christ is never associated with a mower; yet in this poem the traditional scyther, Death, is transmuted into a radiance of spirit, of death overcome, just as loss and loneliness are transformed into living energy. The mower is no longer visible, but is still a dynamically active presence offering the poet heartfelt companionship and inspiration. The 'leaping tongue of bloom' transports the poet into the silent presence and heart of the one who precedes him, yet with whom, if he can follow the promptings of spirit, he can hold 'brotherly speech'. As Steiner says in extract 6 of this volume:

People today need to turn not merely to dead words but to knowledge which actually leads them to the light in which the living Christ dwells: not the historical figure who dwelt on earth centuries ago, but the Christ who lives now and will live through all future times among human beings, because he who was once their God has become their divine brother ...

The poet finds 'a spirit kindred to my own', and whatever name we give this healing, beneficent spirit, the sudden, unexpected companionship leads the tongue of bloom to blossom on Frost's own tongue in language of extraordinary potency and affirmation.

Here is the poem:

I went to turn the grass once after one
Who mowed it in the dew before the sun.

The dew was gone that made his blade so keen
Before I came to view the levelled scene.

I looked for him behind an isle of trees;
I listened for his whetstone on the breeze.

But he had gone his way, the grass all mown,
And I must be, as he had been—alone,

'As all must be,' I said within my heart,
'Whether they work together or apart.'

But as I said it, swift there passed me by
On noiseless wing a bewildered butterfly,

Seeking with memories grown dim o'er night
Some resting flower of yesterday's delight.

And once I marked his flight go round and
    round,
As where some flower lay withering on the
    ground.

And then he flew as far as eye could see,
And then on tremulous wing came back to me.

I thought of questions that have no reply,
And would have turned to toss the grass to dry;

But he turned first, and led my eye to look
At a tall tuft of flowers beside a brook,

A leaping tongue of bloom the scythe had spared
Beside a reedy brook the scythe had bared.

The mower in the dew had loved them thus,
By leaving them to flourish, not for us,

Nor yet to draw one thought of ours to him.
But from sheer morning gladness at the brim.

The butterfly and I had lit upon,
Nevertheless, a message from the dawn,

That made me hear the wakening birds around,
And hear his long scythe whispering to the
  ground,

And feel a spirit kindred to my own;
So that henceforth I worked no more alone;

But glad with him, I worked as with his aid,
And weary, sought at noon with him the shade;

And dreaming, as it were, held brotherly speech
With one whose thought I had not hoped to
  reach.

'Men work together,' I told him from the heart,
'Whether they work together or apart.'

Notes

1. T. S. Eliot, *The Four Quartets*, Faber, 2001.
2. Quoted by Seamus Heaney in 'Craft and Technique', reprinted in: W. N. Herbert and Matthew Hollis, *Strong Words, Modern Poets on Modern Poetry*, Bloodaxe Books, 2000.
3. Take a torch, shut out all other light, and shine the torchlight on paper. The 'beam' of the torch only appears on the paper and where there is dust in the atmosphere to catch it.
4. In Steiner's view we possess, apart from our mineralized physical body, an etheric or life body which we share with the plant kingdom, and an astral or soul body, related to the stars and cosmos, which we have in common with animals. The etheric body is chiefly associated with rhythms, circulation and habitual ways of doing things, while the astral body is the seat of passions, emotions and soul. The fourth and eternal aspect of our being is the 'I' or ego, which continues to exist after death and subsequently seeks reincarnation in a new body. Apart from the physical body, of course, none of the other bodies are visible to sensory perception. One way to gain a sense of their reality is to try to imagine their absence. Without the etheric or life body, for example, a human being could not live and breathe, since the physical body alone is

composed of mineral substance—which is all that is left at death.

5. Anthroposophy was the name Steiner gave to his wide-ranging, Christ-centred philosophy and practice. Literally it means 'wisdom of the human being'.

6. See note 1 above.

7. See companion volume on Easter.

8. The Atlantean epoch of earth's evolution was the fourth epoch, following the Polarian, Hyperborian and Lemurian epochs. It ended with the 'Great Flood' and we are now in the fifth or 'post-Atlantean' era, the midpoint of which was embodied in Greek and Roman culture and the time of Christ. After this fifth epoch, which will end with the 'war of all against all', two further epochs will follow before the dissolution of the earth and its entry into 'pralaya' prior to a new planetary incarnation.

9. One of the core tenets of Steiner's anthroposophy is that we pass through many lives and thus experience a wide range of different cultures and ages in the course of our evolution. The lessons from each life are processed by our eternal essence or ego, and form the basis for each new incarnation.

10. Lucifer and Ahriman are the two polar forces of evil in Steiner's cosmology. Lucifer tempts us away from the earth while Ahriman fetters us to it. Christ is the balancing mediator between these two.

11. See note 1 above.

12. See note 1 above.

13. See note 2 above.

14. See note 1 above.

15. In a recent programme on UK television, a Scotsman showed how his family preserved the memory of their genealogy back to the fifteenth century by reciting the names of forebears. This kind of oral memory still lives on here and there in remote places.

16. See note 1 above. Where the physical body no longer 'interferes' with the etheric and astral realm, our perception of these realms changes. See the original lecture for the full context of this passage, without which it is hard to comprehend.

17. A future stage of angelic consciousness.

18. See note 5 above.

19. See note 1 above.

20. See note 1 above.

21. See note 7 above.

22. Mabel Collins (1851–1927), *Light on the Path*, Theosophical University Press, Pasadena, California.

23. The founders of Rome, Romulus and Remus, were suckled by a wolf.

24. Steiner is here referring to ideas he was promoting for a 'threefold social order'.

25. See note 1 above.

26. 'The Tuft of Flowers' is taken from *The Poetry of Robert Frost*, edited by Edward Connery Lathem and published by Jonathan Cape. Reprinted by permission of The Random House Group Ltd.

Sources

Numbers relate to extract numbers in this volume.

1. Dornach, 7 May 1923, in: *The Festivals and Their Meaning*, Rudolf Steiner Press, 2002.
2. Berlin, 23 May 1904, in: *The Temple Legend*, Rudolf Steiner Press, 2002.
3. Dornach, 7 May 1923, in: *The Festivals and Their Meaning*, Rudolf Steiner Press, 2002.
4. Berlin, 6 June 1916, in: *The Festivals and Their Meaning*, Rudolf Steiner Press, 2002.
5. Berlin, 23 May 1904, in: *The Temple Legend*, Rudolf Steiner Press, 2002.
6. Christiania (Oslo), 17 May 1923, in: *The Festivals and Their Meaning*, Rudolf Steiner Press, 2002.
7. Cologne, 7 June 1908, in: *The Festivals and Their Meaning*, Rudolf Steiner Press, 2002.
8. Dornach, 9 May 1923 in: *From Limestone to Lucifer*, Rudolf Steiner Press, 1999.
9. Dornach, 16 May 1920, in: *Mystery of the Universe*, Rudolf Steiner Press, 2001.
10. Dornach, 4 June 1924, in: *The Festivals and Their Meaning*, Rudolf Steiner Press, 2002.
11. Berlin, 5 June 1905, in: *The Temple Legend*, Rudolf Steiner Press, 2002.

12. Stuttgart, 8 June 1919, in: SA48: typescript in Rudolf
    Steiner Library archive, London.
13. Hamburg, Whit Sunday, 15 May 1910, in: *The Festivals
    and Their Meaning*, Rudolf Steiner Press, 2002.

Further reading

Rudolf Steiner's fundamental books:

Knowledge of the Higher Worlds
also published as: *How to Know Higher Worlds*

Occult Science
also published as: *An Outline of Esoteric Science*

Theosophy

The Philosophy of Freedom
also published as:
Intuitive Thinking as a Spiritual Path

Some relevant volumes of Rudolf Steiner's lectures:

Christmas
Easter
Michaelmas
St John's

The Four Seasons and the Archangels

For all titles contact Rudolf Steiner Press (UK) or
SteinerBooks (USA):
www.rudolfsteinerpress.com www.steinerbooks.org

Note Regarding Rudolf Steiner's Lectures

The lectures and addresses contained in this volume have been translated from the German, which is based on stenographic and other recorded texts that were in most cases never seen or revised by the lecturer. Hence, due to human errors in hearing and transcription, they may contain mistakes and faulty passages. Every effort has been made to ensure that this is not the case. Some of the lectures were given to audiences more familiar with anthroposophy; these are the so-called 'private' or 'members' lectures. Other lectures, like the written works, were intended for the general public. The difference between these, as Rudolf Steiner indicates in his *Autobiography*, is twofold. On the one hand, the members' lectures take for granted a background in and commitment to anthroposophy; in the public lectures this was not the case. At the same time, the members' lectures address the concerns and dilemmas of the members, while the public work speaks directly out of Steiner's own understanding of universal needs. Nevertheless, as Rudolf Steiner stresses: 'Nothing was ever said that was not solely the result of my direct experience of the growing content of anthroposophy. There was never any question of concessions to the prejudices and preferences of the members. Whoever reads these privately printed lectures can take them to represent anthroposophy in the fullest sense. Thus it was possible without hesitation—when the complaints in this direction became too persistent—to depart from the custom of circulating this material "For members only". But it must be borne in mind that faulty passages do occur in these reports not revised by myself.' Earlier in the same chapter, he states: 'Had I been able to correct them [the private lectures], the restriction *for members only* would have been unnecessary from the beginning.'

The original German editions on which this text is based were published by Rudolf Steiner Verlag, Dornach, Switzerland in the collected edition (*Gesamtausgabe*, 'GA') of Rudolf Steiner's work. All publications are edited by the Rudolf Steiner Nachlassverwaltung (estate), which wholly owns both Rudolf Steiner Verlag and the Rudolf Steiner Archive. The organization relies solely on donations to continue its activity.

Rudolf Steiner
Easter
An Introductory Reader

Chapters: Can we Celebrate Easter?; The Earth and the
Cosmos; Rising Sun, Nature and Resurrection; Golgotha,
the Central Deed of Evolution; Easter, a Festival for the
Future.

160pp; 978 185584 139 0; £6.99

Rudolf Steiner
St John's
An Introductory Reader

Chapters: Midsummer Dream, the Earth Breathes Out;
Finding the Greater Self; 'He Must Increase, I Must
Decrease'; Creating Vision.

112pp; 978 185584 174 1; £5.99

Rudolf Steiner
Michaelmas
An Introductory Reader

Chapters: Sinking Earth, Rising Spirit; Michael and the
Dragon; Michael, Spirit of Our Age; Towards a Michael
Festival.

160pp; 978 185584 159 8; £6.99

Rudolf Steiner
Christmas
An Introductory Reader

Chapters: Christmas in a Grievous Age; Christmas and
the Earth; Delving to the Core; The Child and the Tree;
Towards a New Christmas.

168pp; 978 185584 189 5; £6.99